DATE DUE

VALERIE BODDEN

grow with me

SPIDER

CREATIVE EDUCATION

Published by Creative Education
P.O. Box 227, Mankato, Minnesota 56002
Creative Education is an imprint of
The Creative Company
www.thecreativecompany.us

Design by Ellen Huber
Production by Chelsey Luther
Art direction by Rita Marshall
Printed in the United States of America

Photographs by Alamy (Vicki Beaver), Dreamstime
(Cathy Keifer, Nicco99, Teh Soon Huat, Tomatito26),
National Geographic Stock (JESSE BUTT, MARK
W. MOFFETT, AMY WHITE & AL PETTEWAY),
Shutterstock (alstutksy, Eric Isselee, Cathy Keifer,
Kletr, D. Kucharski K. Kucharska, MarkMirror, somyot
pattana, Panu Ruangjan, Tomatito, Peter Waters),
SuperStock (Biosphoto, FLPA, George Grall/National
Geographic, imagebroker.net, Minden Pictures,
NaturePL, NHPA, Patricia Vasquez)

Library of Congress Cataloging-in-Publication Data
Bodden, Valerie.
Spider / Valerie Bodden.
p. cm. — (Grow with me)
Includes bibliographical references and index.
Summary: An exploration of the life cycle and life
span of spiders, using up-close photographs and step-
by-step text to follow a spider's growth process from
egg to spiderling to mature spider.

ISBN 978-1-60818-407-1
1. Spiders—Juvenile literature. 2. Spiders—Life cycles—
Juvenile literature. I. Title.
QL458.4.B65 2014
595.4'4—dc23   2013029625

CCSS: RI.3.1, 2, 3, 4, 5, 6, 7, 8; RI.4.1, 2, 3, 4, 5, 7; RF.3.3, 4

9 8 7 6 5 4 3

TABLE OF CONTENTS

Spiders are arachnids. Arachnids are animals with eight legs and two body sections. The cephalothorax (*SEF-uh-luh-THOR-aks*) contains the eyes, mouth, and legs. The abdomen (*AB-doh-mun*) holds the spider's **organs** and **silk glands**.

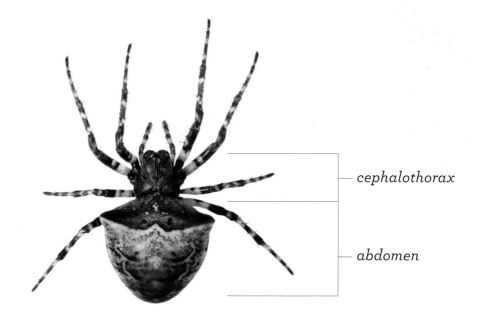

cephalothorax

abdomen

Spiders can be found everywhere on Earth except Antarctica. They make their homes in forests, grasslands, deserts, caves, and even people's homes. Scientists have found more than 40,000 spider **species**.

4

A spider's mouthparts
are called chelicerae
(kuh-LIS-eh-ray).

5

6 Jumping spiders have four pairs of eyes, but some are on top of the head.

The smallest spiders are less than a quarter of an inch (0.6 cm) long. But the biggest tarantulas (*tuh-RAN-choo-luhz*) can be as big as a grown-up's hand! Most spiders are black or brown to blend in with their surroundings. But some are bright red, yellow, or orange.

Most spiders have eight eyes. But they cannot see very well. A spider's body is covered with lots of small hairs. The hairs pick up **vibrations**. A spider also has two "feelers" called pedipalps at the sides of its mouth.

7

pedipalps

All spiders have organs called spinnerets. The spider uses them to spin silk. The silk starts as a liquid in the spider's body. When it comes out of the spinnerets, it dries into a solid thread.

Many spiders use their silk to make webs. Some spiders use silk to line burrows, or dens. Whenever a spider moves, it sticks a piece of silk called a dragline to a sturdy object. The dragline will catch the spider if it falls or jumps.

Orb weaver spiders do not have good eyesight. They spin webs by touch.

The biggest webs can be 80 feet (24 m) wide and cross rivers.

9

Female spiders use silk to protect their eggs. A spider lays 1 to 1,000 or more eggs at a time. The spider wraps the eggs in a **cocoon** of silk called an egg sac.

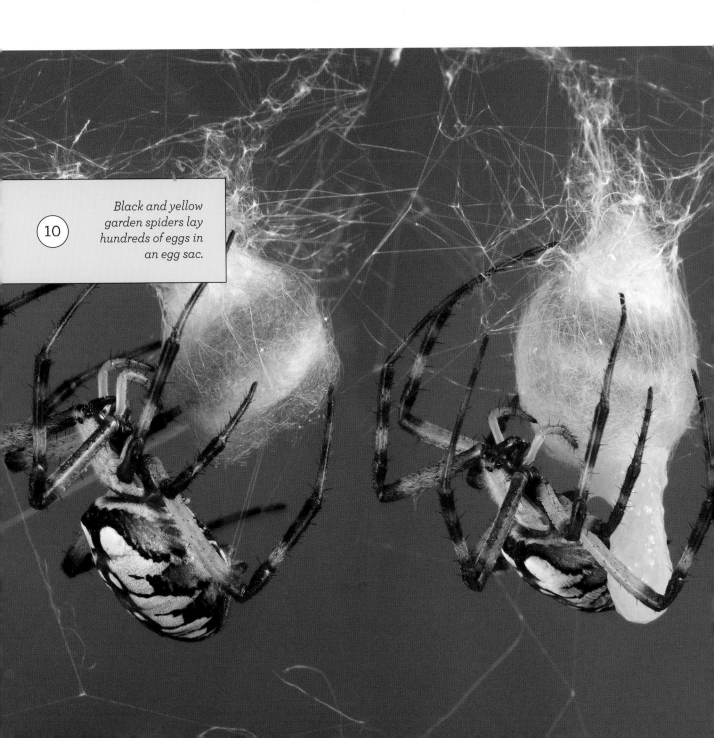

10

Black and yellow garden spiders lay hundreds of eggs in an egg sac.

The egg sac keeps the spider eggs safe from **insects** and other spiders. A baby spider inside an egg is called an **embryo** (*EM-bree-oh*). The embryo gets food from the egg's **yolk**.

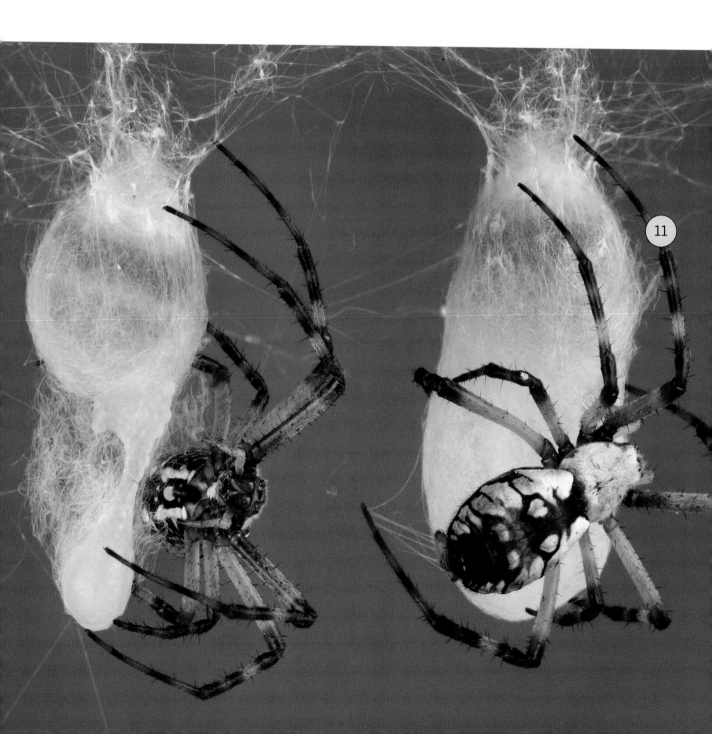

Most spiders develop in their eggs for about two or three weeks before they hatch. But in some cold places, spiders stay in their eggs over the winter. They will hatch the next spring.

All the eggs in the egg sac hatch at the same time. The young spiders, called spiderlings, look like tiny adult spiders. The spiderlings stay in the egg sac after they hatch. They come out after they **molt** once or twice.

12

Many kinds of spiders lay eggs that stick together into a partly built sac.

Young wolf spiders grow to become night-time hunters with excellent eyesight.

Wolf spiders carry their egg sacs. The hatched young ride on their mothers.

A mother spider may eat an insect and feed spiderlings liquid from her mouth.

15

Most mother spiders do not take care of their babies. But a few kinds of spiders stay with the spiderlings for a week or two. They protect the spiderlings and find them food.

Some mother spiders take care of the spiderlings in a burrow. Others build a silk web around the spiderlings. Some spiders carry their babies on their back.

Wasp spiders hatch in the fall but stay in the sac until spring.

(16) Most spiderlings do not stay together very long. They might start to eat each other! Some kinds of spiders walk away to find new homes.

Other kinds of spiders balloon to new places. They stand on something tall, such as a blade of grass. Then they lift their abdomen into the air and let out a line of silk. The silk is picked up by the wind. The spiderling gets carried along with it.

When spiders balloon, they cannot control how far they travel.

17

18 *Young golden orb-weavers do not have yellow-colored silk like adults do.*

A spiderling's exoskeleton (*EK-so-SKEL-ih-tin*), or shell, cannot grow, so the spider has to molt. To molt, a spiderling lies on its back or hangs from a strand of silk. Its old shell splits open, and the spiderling wriggles out. Its new shell is soft at first. This helps the spiderling grow bigger.

It can take a few hours or a few days for a spiderling's shell to harden. During this time, the spiderling is in danger from **predators**. It cannot move or defend itself. Most spiderlings molt 3 to 10 times before becoming adults.

19

Birds with long bills, such as kingfishers, can snatch spiders for food.

Even when it is not molting, a spider faces threats from many predators. Many kinds of insects eat spiders. So do birds, centipedes, and other spiders.

Most spiders do not fight their enemies. They run away instead. Tarantulas might raise their front legs and show their **fangs** to scare an enemy.

20

Huntsman spiders look threatening, but they tend to bite only insects.

Insects such as mantises wait for a spider to come close enough to grab.

21

Some spiders wrap prey in silk to store it for later eating.

22

Some spiders spend their time hunting for **prey**. Others catch their prey in a web. The largest spiders can eat birds, mice, or frogs!

A spider bites its prey with its fangs. The fangs send **venom** into the prey. The venom kills the prey or makes it unable to move. Then the spider sends chemicals into the prey's body. The chemicals turn the body into a liquid that the spider sucks up.

23

A spider's venom allows it to take on prey larger than itself.

The female flower crab spider is more than twice the size of a male.

A spider is fully grown once it has finished molting. This takes some spiders only a few weeks or months. Spiders that live a long time might not be fully grown for 10 years.

24

Once a male spider becomes an adult, it looks for a female mate. Some male spiders raise their legs into the air to attract a female. Other males tap on the ground or on a web to make vibrations that "call" a female. Some males bring food.

26 *Cave spiders in Europe make stretchy silk to hang egg sacs from cave ceilings.*

After mating, many male spiders die. Sometimes the female eats them! Other male spiders just leave.

The female spider waits one to two weeks to lay her eggs. She wraps them in an egg sac. Some females hang the sac from a leaf or bury it. Others guard the sac or carry it with them.

27

Nursery web spiders carry egg sacs using their jaws and pedipalps.

Most spiders have six spinnerets. Some have two, four, or eight.

(28) Many female spiders live only a few months. But females of big species can live 20 years. Most female spiders die after laying their eggs. The eggs they left behind will soon hatch. New spiderlings will molt and grow to weave their own webs.

29

A female spider lays 1 to 1,000 eggs and wraps them in an egg sac.

An embryo begins to grow in each egg.

In about 2 weeks (or the next spring), the egg hatches.

The spiderling molts 1 or 2 times in the egg sac.

After a few days, the spiderling walks or balloons away from the egg sac.

The spiderling molts for the last time when it is a few weeks to 10 years old.

The spider finds a mate.  Many males die after mating.

A female spider lays her eggs 1 to 2 weeks after mating.

When it is a few months to 20 years old, the spider dies.

cocoon: *a case or covering made of silk*

embryo: *an offspring that has not hatched out of an egg yet*

fangs: *in spiders, the biting parts of the mouth*

glands: *parts of the body that make chemicals needed by the body*

insects: *animals that have six legs and one or two pairs of wings*

molt: *to lose an old skin and grow a new one*

organs: *parts of an animal's body that do certain jobs*

predators: *animals that kill and eat other animals*

prey: *animals that are killed and eaten by other animals*

species: *groups of living things that are closely related*

venom: *a poison made by an animal such as a spider*

vibrations: *back-and-forth movements*

yolk: *the middle, yellow part of an egg that contains food for a growing embryo*

31

WEBSITES

Enchanted Learning: Spiders
http://www.enchantedlearning.com/subjects/arachnids/spider/
Spiderprintout.shtml
Learn more about spiders and print out a picture of a spider to color.

Kidzone: Spiders
http://www.kidzone.ws/lw/spiders/index.htm
Check out spider activities, facts, and pictures.

Note: Every effort has been made to ensure that the websites listed above are suitable for children, that they have educational value, and that they contain no inappropriate material. However, because of the nature of the Internet, it is impossible to guarantee that these sites will remain active indefinitely or that their contents will not be altered.

READ MORE

Bodden, Valerie. *Spiders*.
Mankato, Minn.: Creative Education, 2011.

Halfmann, Janet. *Spiders*.
Mankato, Minn.: Creative Education, 2002.

(32)